GERTRUDE
ELION

Master Chemist

Stephanie St. Pierre

D1127505

ROURKE ENTERPRISES,INC.
VERO BEACH, FLORIDA 32964

© 1993 Rourke Enterprises, Inc.

A Blackbirch Graphics Book.

Library of Congress Cataloging-in-Publication Data

St. Pierre, Stephanie.
    Gertrude Elion / by Stephanie St. Pierre.
        p.   cm. — (Masters of invention)
    Includes bibliographic references.
    Includes index.
    Summary: A biography of the chemist who, in recognition of her important discoveries and inventions, was the first woman inducted into the National Inventors Hall of Fame.
    ISBN 0-86592-130-X
    1. Elion, Gertrude B.—Juvenile literature. 2. Pharmaceutical chemistry—United States—Biography—Juvenile literature. 3. Women chemists—United States—Biography—Juvenile literature.
[1. Elion, Gertrude B. 2. Chemists. 3. Inventors.] I. Title.
II. Series.
RS403.S74   1993
615'.19'0092—dc20
[B]   93-22315
                                                              CIP
                                                              AC

CONTENTS

Chapter One   A Life-Saving Inventor   *5*

Chapter Two   A Woman with Purpose   *10*

Chapter Three   Job Hunting   *20*

Chapter Four   Forty Years of Important Work   *27*

Chapter Five   Life after Burroughs Wellcome   *39*

Glossary   *46*

For Further Reading   *46*

Index   *47*

A LIFE-SAVING INVENTOR

"How you handle setbacks can make a difference."

*A*lthough you have probably never heard of her, Gertrude Belle Elion is a scientist whose discoveries have greatly affected all our lives. In 1991, when she became the first woman to be named to the National Inventors Hall of Fame, Gertrude was surprised. She had always thought of herself as a researcher, not an inventor. "But I guess I had invented new compounds—and then had to discover what they were good for," Gertrude said when asked about the honor.

A Chemist at Burroughs Wellcome

For almost 40 years Gertrude worked as a chemist and researcher for Burroughs Wellcome, a large pharmaceutical company.

Opposite: Gertrude Elion has dedicated her life to fighting diseases thought to be incurable. Over the years, her research has saved thousands of lives.

Gertrude first met George Hitchings in 1944. The two scientists formed a working partnership that lasted for forty years.

Pharmaceuticals are drugs that are specifically used to treat disease; in other words, they are medicines. At Burroughs Wellcome, Gertrude helped to create new treatments for diseases that hundreds of thousands of people all over the world had. Even drugs that Gertrude did not invent herself were developed as a result of her research.

One of the most important drugs that Gertrude researched (along with her partner of many years, Dr. George Hitchings) is a drug called Imuran. At first Gertrude developed the drug to fight cancer. But, in fact, it didn't work much better than drugs that were already available. This was disappointing. Some people would have let such disappointment stop them, but not Gertrude.

"Research is very hard work," remarks Gertrude. "There's no other way, but how you handle setbacks can make a difference. In science, you have to take several approaches to setbacks. You just have to say to yourself that you've tried everything, it didn't work, so I have to go a different direction....You must never feel that you have failed. You can always come back to something later, when you have more knowledge or better equipment, and try again. I've done this and it worked!"

Hard Work Pays Off

Although Imuran did not help fight cancer, Gertrude kept working with it until she found a use for it. Eventually, she discovered that Imuran could be helpful in organ transplants. In a transplant operation, a doctor replaces a diseased organ, such as a kidney, with a healthy organ from another body.

Doctors had been trying to do successful organ transplants for years but there was one big problem. Once the operation was over, the body realized that the new organ did not belong. It would attack the organ, except in

Gertrude posed with the dog who successfully accepted a kidney transplant after taking Imuran—a drug Gertrude researched.

the case of identical twins, who have the same type of tissue in their bodies.

In the course of her experimentation with Imuran, Gertrude realized that the drug could prevent the foreign organ from being attacked by the body. Doctors had previously tried to use other drugs when doing organ transplants to accomplish this, but Gertrude and her partner thought that Imuran would work better. They were right.

In 1960, Gertrude decided to use a collie dog named Lollipop to test out Imuran. The dog was given a new kidney, using the new drug. Lollipop lived for 230 days—almost an entire year—before dying of an illness that was not related to the transplant. Soon, doctors were using Imuran during human transplant operations. Gertrude's hard work and inventiveness had paid off.

It took some time to figure out what the best dosages (amounts given) and procedures should be when using Imuran. But after three years of research, Imuran proved to be an extremely useful tool for doctors who performed organ transplants. Still widely in use today, the drug has saved thousands of lives.

Imuran is only one of the many important drugs for which Gertrude has been credited. Through her hard work, determination, and discipline, Gertrude has overcome great obstacles and has made life for all of us a little easier. And Gertrude herself knows that it was worth all the effort. "When you meet someone who has lived for twenty-five years with a kidney graft, there's your reward."

Over the years, Gertrude has received many distinct awards and honors, including the Nobel Prize, the most important award given to scientists. This is the story of Gertrude Elion's life and work as a pioneering scientist and crusading inventor.

CHAPTER TWO

A WOMAN WITH PURPOSE

"I always wanted a job where you didn't stop learning and there was always something new."

*G*ertrude Belle Elion was born on January 23, 1918, in New York City. She spent the first seven years of her life in Manhattan with her mother, a housewife, and her father, a dentist. Her brother, Herbert, was born when she was five years old.

About the time that she turned seven, Gertrude's family moved to another part of New York City, in the Bronx, called the Grand Concourse. It was a lovely area. There were nice houses and large apartment buildings surrounded by trees. Gertrude and her friends played games in an empty lot near her house and she walked to school every day.

Gertrude, three-and-a-half years old, enjoys a cold winter's day with her mother in 1921.

A Young Scientist Grows Up Quickly

Gertrude was a good student. She loved to read and was always curious about everything. Although science was not a special interest of hers, one of Gertrude's favorite books was Paul de Kruif's *Microbe Hunters.* It tells the story of many famous scientists and their great discoveries. It was an important book for Gertrude because it made science come alive. The stories of the scientists' discoveries made a life of research sound exciting. As an adult, Gertrude said that she thought every child should read de Kruif's book to get a good idea of what it was really like to be a scientist.

Because she was very smart, Gertrude skipped ahead into higher grades four times during her early years. This was good in some ways. She always had new things to learn and didn't get bored. In other ways, however, it was hard. When she started high school at the age of 12, Gertrude had very different interests than the other girls in her grade. Most of her classmates were two or three years older than she. The older girls were thinking about going on dates and meeting boys. But Gertrude wasn't quite ready for that yet.

During these years, Gertrude found most of her comfort and satisfaction in learning. She studied Latin and French, and got very good marks in English. When she was an

Even as a small child, Gertrude's eagerness to learn was apparent. She loved to read and was curious about everything.

adult and spoke with some of her old high school teachers, everyone was surprised that Gertrude had become a scientist. Her teachers had expected her to be a writer or historian because English and history were two of her favorite subjects. But when Gertrude graduated from high school at the age of 15, she wasn't sure what she wanted to do. It was a very uncertain and difficult time for her.

An Important Decision

About the time Gertrude graduated from high school, her grandfather, whom she loved very much, died of cancer. Suddenly, Gertrude knew what she wanted to do. She decided that she would find a cure for cancer. It was a big decision and one that she stuck with for the rest of her life. "When I was fifteen, I already knew from my high school courses

Gertrude graduated from high school when she was only 15. Her hard work and natural abilities allowed her to skip grades four times in school.

that I loved science," Gertrude explains. "But
that year I was so devastated [upset] by my
grandfather's death from cancer that majoring
in chemistry seemed the logical first step in
committing myself to fighting the disease."

Gertrude wanted to learn more about the
awful disease that had taken her grandfather's
life. She wanted to work toward finding a way
to save others from cancer. "I felt very strongly
that I had a motive, a goal in life that I could
try to do something about," Gertrude said
when asked about her decision to become a
scientist at such an early age.

Gertrude attended Hunter College, in New
York City. She planned to study chemistry to
learn about the basic substances that make up
life. Keeping in mind her goal to find a cure
for cancer, Gertrude might have chosen to
study biology. Gertrude, however, did not
want to cut up animals. Dissection (cutting
open dead animals to learn about how they
work inside) is an important part of the study
of biology. It is not, however, necessary for
the study of chemistry.

Although research jobs in chemistry were
not normally open to women in the 1930s,
Gertrude still continued to see herself as a
cancer researcher. At that time, most women
who earned degrees in the sciences were expected to go on to become nurses or teachers.
Gertrude was clearly not like most women.

In 1933, Gertrude decided that she would study chemistry at Hunter College in New York City.

She chose the college courses that would best prepare her for a research job. Out of about 75 women majoring in chemistry in Gertrude's class, only 6 or 7 went on to become science researchers.

Gertrude's father had hoped that she and her brother would follow in his footsteps and become dentists. Although Gertrude did not want to be a dentist, she still made her parents happy by choosing to become a scientist. They were a source of great encouragement for her. Her brother, Herbert, became a physicist and an engineer.

Gertrude worked very hard in college. When she looked for another woman to compare herself with, she thought of Madame Curie. Gertrude had read many books about Madame Curie, who was one of the first important women scientists. Her example was inspirational. It was important for Gertrude to realize that other women had succeeded in their dreams of becoming scientific researchers.

At Hunter College during the 1930s, many exciting and new things were being discovered in the field of physics. Although physics was not Gertrude's major area of study, it was included in her course work. But the physics that was being taught in standard courses did not include the breakthroughs of the day. Gertrude learned about the new findings with the help of an exceptional professor, Dr. Otis.

Recognizing that a small group of the women in his class wanted to become serious scientists, Dr. Otis set up a special study group. The young women would meet at Dr. Otis's home to discuss articles that Dr. Otis had given them from scholarly journals. In this way, Dr. Otis kept them up-to-date on the most important scientific happenings of the day. The interest that this professor showed his students made a deep impression on Gertrude. She would try to do the same for her own students.

Gertrude worked hard in college. She often met with other female students to discuss current scientific theories and data. Dr. Otis, one of Gertrude's mentors, helped lead the discussions.

After college, when Gertrude was teaching physics in high school, she amazed a student who tried to stump her with difficult physics questions. The student had gotten the questions from his college-age brother who was a physics major. When Gertrude responded to the questions without hesitating, the student was stunned. He could not believe that this young, inexperienced high school teacher understood such complex matters.

Breaking Into a "Man's Field"

It was 1937 when Gertrude graduated from college summa cum laude (with very high honors) with a bachelor's degree in chemistry.

It was not a particularly good year in America, or anywhere else in the world. World War II would soon break out in Europe. All over the world, people were suffering from poverty because there weren't enough jobs. Women especially had very few opportunities.

Women were expected to marry, to raise children, and to care for a home. Teaching, secretarial work, and nursing were the only jobs regularly available to them. It was a most difficult time to be a young woman trying to break into a "man's" field. The fact that Gertrude did not give up her plans to become a chemist shows how deeply devoted she was to her goal and how much she truly loved science.

Gertrude was courageous to follow her dream. She knew that she must continue her education. But she also needed a job to pay for it. In 1937, she began interviewing, hoping to land a good research job that would pay enough so that she could return to school at some point. College had only made her more sure of her goals.

"Science is the kind of discipline where you keep learning all the time," Gertrude says. "I always wanted a job where you didn't stop learning and there was always something new." It would take some time and a great deal of patience, however, before Gertrude finally found that job.

CHAPTER THREE

JOB HUNTING

*"It wasn't until men went to war. . .that
they finally found they needed me!"*

Despite her excellent
record at Hunter College, Gertrude had a very
hard time finding a job as a researcher. She
interviewed at numerous laboratories, but all
rejected her. She remembers one rejection in
particular. She was sure the interview had
gone well, but as it was nearing the end, the
interviewer told her that he couldn't hire her
because she was too attractive and would be a
distraction to the other workers who were, of
course, all men. "It surprises me that I didn't
get angry," says Gertrude. "I got very discour-
aged. But how could I...know what the men
were like?"

A Difficult Beginning

Desperate for work Gertrude took a six-week
secretarial course so that she would have more
acceptable skills for a woman. Finally, she got

Although Gertrude was successful at Hunter College, she had a difficult time finding a research job after graduation. She experienced discrimination because she was a woman.

a three-month job with the New York Hospital School of Nursing. She taught nurses how to work in the laboratory. It was not exactly the beginning she had hoped for, but Gertrude was not going to quit trying. When she met a man who offered to give her an unpaid job working in his laboratory, she took it. After a while, Gertrude was paid $12 a week, not much to get by on, even in those days. After six months, she was making $20 a week, which still wasn't very much—"slave wages" as Gertrude later commented.

Most scientists have to go to school for a long time to be good researchers. After getting a bachelor's degree, they must do further study to get a master's degree. Most then go on for an even more advanced degree, called a doctorate, or Ph.D. There are many talented and brilliant scientists who have succeeded without a Ph.D. Not having one, however, often makes it difficult to get ahead in the scientific community.

Gertrude knew that she needed to go back to school in order to advance as a researcher. By saving what she could of her small salary and by living at home with her parents, Gertrude eventually managed to get enough money together to continue her studies. She was determined.

She enrolled in New York University (NYU) and began working toward her master's degree in chemistry. In the mornings, she worked as a receptionist in a doctor's office to pay for her schooling, books, and other needs. She spent her first year taking courses. During her second year, she did research. By that time Gertrude had begun teaching chemistry and physics in New York City public high schools. At night and on weekends, she did her research at NYU. It was an exhausting schedule but worth the price. In 1941, she received her degree. Again, she began interviewing for scientific research jobs.

A Changed Job Market

Things were different in the job market in 1941. America was fighting World War II. With most men off to war, there was suddenly a variety of job openings for women. It took a while, but this time Gertrude found a job that was more suited to her. When an employment agency called to ask if Gertrude was still interested in laboratory work, Gertrude jumped at the chance to begin her career doing research.

"Interested???" asked Gertrude. "Of course I was still interested! It was all I ever wanted to do. It wasn't until men went to war, though, that they finally found they needed me! War changed everything. Whatever reservations there were about employing women in laboratories simply evaporated."

Gertrude's first laboratory job was working for A&P, the grocery-store chain, in Brooklyn, New York. At first, she found the job interesting. Everything about it was new. At A&P, Gertrude was able to learn about new instruments used for experimentation. After a time, however, checking the acidity of pickles, the color of mayonnaise, and the mold content in berries for jam began to get tiresome. A year and a half later, Gertrude decided that she had learned enough at A&P. She knew that in order to be happy, she had to move on.

Gertrude soon found a new job as an assistant in a pharmaceutical laboratory at the Johnson & Johnson company. The job looked promising, but after only a few months the company decided to shut down the research division. Gertrude was offered another job at Johnson & Johnson, testing the strength of surgical sutures—the threads used to sew people up after an operation. It didn't sound like a position that would eventually lead to a cure for cancer. After careful consideration, Gertrude decided not to accept the job.

Finally, a Break

Once again, Gertrude was looking for work. She was 26 years old. It was 1944, and America was still at war, so the shortage of men to fill jobs was worse than ever. Gertrude

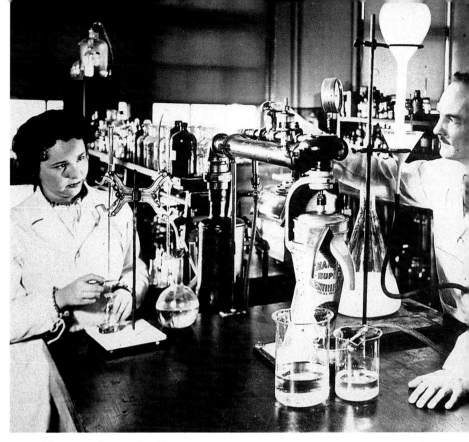

In 1944, Gertrude was finally given the opportunity to do the laboratory research she had always dreamed of doing. She was hired by Burroughs Wellcome, a pharmaceutical company in Tuckahoe, New York.

was offered several different jobs, but none of them seemed quite right. She knew what she wanted—she just had to go out to find it. And that she did.

One day, as Gertrude was looking at the label on a bottle of Empirin, a pain reliever, she noticed the name *Burroughs Wellcome* printed on it. She had an idea. She would call the company to ask if it had an opening for a laboratory assistant.

Soon after she made that call, Gertrude put on her best suit and went down to Burroughs

Wellcome for an interview. As she walked through the building on her way to see George Hitchings, she noticed a woman at work in the lab. This set her at ease. Clearly, she would not be turned away here simply because she was a woman.

Gertrude was quite excited by the work that George Hitchings described. "I didn't understand half of what he was saying, but his description of his work so enthralled me that I knew then and there that I'd give my life to finding out about it." Little did she knew that George would be her working partner for the next 40 years!

FORTY YEARS OF IMPORTANT WORK

"What greater joy can you have than to know what an impact your work has on people's lives?"

*B*urroughs Wellcome has always had a special approach to the pharmaceutical business. From the time it was founded in England in 1894 by a man named Henry Wellcome, the company's philosophy has been to search for drugs to treat serious incurable diseases. It has never been known as a company that manufactures medicines just to make money.

A Partner for Life

George Hitchings joined Burroughs Wellcome just two years before hiring Gertrude as his assistant. Like her, his early interest in science

was the result of the death of someone close to him. When George was 12 years old, his father died. And, just as Gertrude had been inspired by Madame Curie, George had been inspired by the famous scientist Louis Pasteur.

For 12 years after getting his Ph.D. in chemistry, George was a university professor. In 1942, he joined Burroughs Wellcome. Soon he was stirring things up with his new style of research. At the time, most pharmaceutical research was done with a certain disease in mind. Scientists would decide to look for a cure for that disease and then begin testing different things to see how they affected the disease. This method is called trial and error. George, however, wanted to do basic research on different kinds of chemicals, collecting information as he went along. He thought that once a scientist better understood the basics about a chemical or compound, he or she would be better prepared to guess at how it might work as a medicine. This is the method used in most laboratories today. By the time George hired Gertrude, he was well known for his different ways of thinking and doing things. No one questioned the fact that he was hiring a young woman who didn't even have a Ph.D. If George thought it was the right thing to do, everyone else went along.

One person who did object to Gertrude's hiring was chemist Elvira Falco—another woman who worked in the lab. "She told him [George] not to hire me because I was too well dressed," Gertrude said. "Well, wouldn't you wear you're best suit for an interview?" she asked. Despite her disapproval of young Gertrude's choice in clothes, Elvira later worked closely and productively with both George and Gertrude until she eventually left the company in the 1950s.

One of Gertrude's first breakthroughs at Burroughs Wellcome was finding a treatment for leukemia, a form of cancer.

When Gertrude joined the company, Burroughs Wellcome was located in Tuckahoe, New York, a small town about 30 miles outside New York City. The office was in an old rubber-factory building. The lab was small and spread over two floors. Gertrude worked on one floor, and George worked on the other. All day long, scientists ran up and down the stairs discussing their findings and new discoveries. It was an exciting place to be, especially for Gertrude. Gertrude was put to work investigating chemical compounds called purines, found in human cells. Scientists hoped that purines might be used as a cancer treatment.

Back to School

Gertrude loved her work and was happy with her new job, but she was worried that she did not have a Ph.D. It is difficult for a person to advance in a scientific career without having an advanced degree, so, Gertrude enrolled in a Ph.D. program in chemistry at Polytechnic University in Brooklyn, New York. Gertrude not only had a demanding full-time job during the day, but now she had to travel two hours to attend her evening classes. Then, she had to again make the tiresome trip to get home. Despite this exhausting schedule, Gertrude was determined to get her Ph.D.

Unfortunately, a dean at the university told Gertrude that he did not think she was serious enough about her studies and suggested that she either become a full-time student or drop out. It was a heartbreaking choice, considering the work she had already put into getting her doctorate. But Gertrude couldn't give up her job. She needed the money, and she realized that the opportunity she had at Burroughs Wellcome was not something she was likely to find again easily, if at all. She kept the job and left Polytechnic University.

A Major Breakthrough

Gertrude's work was going well, yet she continued to worry about not having completed her degree. These worries finally faded when she made her first really important discovery. After many trials, Gertrude uncovered a drug that proved to be effective in treating—but not curing—leukemia, a form of cancer. "All science is a continuous process of bits and pieces of information and knowledge," says Gertrude. In this case, the bits and pieces came together as a treatment for leukemia. The drug, named Purinethol, was the result of years of research with purines.

Purinethol, still in use today, is often used to treat children with leukemia. Although it is not a cure for the disease, it slows the disease

In her forty years at Burroughs Wellcome, Gertrude helped to develop numerous treatments for cancer and various viruses. Her research later inspired work on other drugs as well—namely AZT, used to treat AIDS.

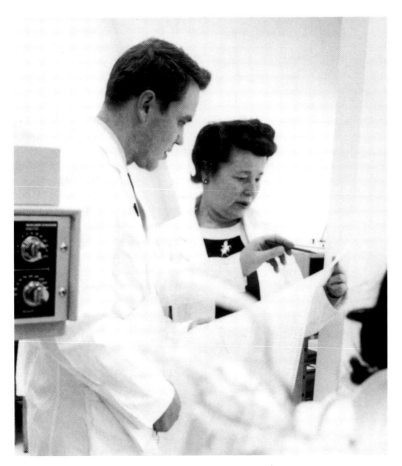

Gertrude's open personality and generous spirit made her a welcome role model for younger scientists.

down and gives children and their doctors more time to fight it. "What greater joy can you have," says Gertrude, "than to know what an impact your work has on people's lives? We get letters from people all the time—from children who are living with leukemia. You can't beat the feeling you get from those children." As the years passed, Gertrude and George worked closely together on many projects. Each time George was promoted to a new job, Gertrude moved into the one he had left.

Over and over again, their research led to new breakthroughs. Sometimes she worked on her own, and sometimes they worked together. Gertrude became an important role model for younger scientists who admired her record of discoveries and her pleasant, open personality. As new researchers entered the laboratory, they were included in the exciting process of discovery. Gertrude enjoyed teaching the new scientists who followed in her path. They were honored to work for her.

At Burroughs Wellcome, Gertrude and other researchers tried to learn as much as they could about different chemicals and compounds.

More Breakthroughs

Gertrude and George wrote many papers that described their research. These papers were published in various scientific magazines and journals. Gertrude read her papers at scientific meetings or at university lectures. Scientists all over the world were thus able to learn what Gertrude and George were doing.

Scientists at Burroughs Wellcome were expected to develop new drugs and patent them. A patent is a kind of license that the government gives to someone who has come up with a new idea, medicine, or machine before anyone else has. It is not easy to get a patent. Gertrude Elion was 45 when she got her first one. In addition to Imuran and Purinethol, Gertrude developed—either on her own or with other scientists—several different medicines for treating cancer and viruses. Her work also opened the way for research into other drugs. One of these drugs, AZT, which was developed after Gertrude's retirement, is used to fight the deadly HIV virus. When people try to credit Gertrude with inspiring the researchers who discovered AZT, she modestly comments, "The only thing I can claim is training people in the methodology; how to delve into how things work and why they don't work and what resistance is and so on. The work was all theirs."

A Move

In 1970, Burroughs Wellcome moved from Tuckahoe, New York, to North Carolina. Even though she had lived all her life in New York City, Gertrude didn't hesitate to move with the company. She would miss her friends and the excitement of New York, including the opera, which she loves, but the choice was simple. "I couldn't bear giving up my job," said Gertrude. "I already had an excellent department and was doing exciting work and I didn't want to leave it."

Soon Gertrude was settling into a cozy townhouse just outside Chapel Hill, a beautiful college town not far from the new home of Burroughs Wellcome. Gertrude never married. At one time she was engaged, but her fiancé died suddenly. It took quite a long time for Gertrude to recover from the loss. She had boyfriends over the years, but no one else made quite the same impression.

Opening the Door for Other Women

When Gertrude was young, though she might have married, it is unlikely that she could have had children and continued in her job. In her day, a woman was often fired if her employer learned that she was pregnant. But even though Gertrude did not have children of her

Together, George Hitchings and Gertrude Elion helped change the way scientific research is done.

own to care for, she has saved the lives of thousands of sick children with the medicines that she discovered.

Luckily, times have changed. Today, a woman cannot be fired just because she has a family. In many ways, it is because of the dedication and hard work of women like Gertrude Elion that women now have greater choices in their lives.

"I certainly do not consider myself a pioneer in the way Madame Curie was a pioneer, although I do consider that I have taken part in a pioneering endeavor," said Gertrude. "Other women have made significant contributions and done particularly well in science, too." Gertrude was most definitely a pioneer in the field of scientific research. But her importance is heightened by the fact that she pioneered as a woman. By making a new place for herself in the field of medical and academic research, Gertrude opened the door for generations of women scientists to come.

LIFE AFTER BURROUGHS WELLCOME

"I've reached a stage where I teach and I'm ready to pass the research torch on to others to carry."

*I*n 1983, after almost 40 years at Burroughs Wellcome, Gertrude decided to retire. She thought retirement would give her more time to work in the lab, pursuing whatever interested her. Instead, Gertrude has kept herself busier than ever. Much of her time has been spent teaching, lecturing, and working for organizations such as the National Cancer Advisory Board and the World Health Organization. Gertrude has also continued to be an important presence at Burroughs Wellcome. She has been known to check up on the progress of experiments, offer advice, and just observe happenings in the lab.

Lab workers have always been glad to see her. A born teacher, Gertrude has had a special ability to fill those around her with the same enthusiasm she brings to her work.

A Doctorate, at Last

Since 1969, Gertrude has received at least 10 honorary doctoral degrees. An honorary degree is awarded to someone for extraordinary achievement in a particular field of study. People who receive such awards never have to attend a class. Clearly, not earning her Ph.D. through course work had not held Gertrude back very much!

The Nobel Prize

On the morning of October 17, 1988, just as Gertrude was about to wash her face, the phone rang. It was a reporter calling to ask her how she felt about winning the Nobel Prize. Gertrude thought it was a joke. She soon learned, however, that the call was for real. She and George Hitchings had won the prize in physiology and medicine for their work in drug research. Nobel prizes are very rarely given to employees of pharmaceutical companies. Maybe this is why the prize came almost 30 years after the team had made its most major discoveries!

In 1988, partners Gertrude Elion and George Hitchings were awarded the Nobel Prize for their contributions to medical research. Out of all those who received awards, Gertrude was the only woman.

Gertrude took 11 members of her family with her to the Nobel Prize ceremony in Stockholm, Sweden. Of all the winners in 1988, Gertrude was the only woman. She looked beautiful in a deep-blue chiffon gown. She stood out like a bright jewel.

It was wonderful for Gertrude to receive such recognition for all her years of hard work. But, when asked if getting the award was the best thing that ever happened in her career, Gertrude replied, "Of course not!...We had our reward with all our drugs, and this [the Nobel Prize] is very nice, but you don't work for this. I mean if you didn't get it, you would have wasted your whole life!"

Other Awards

Gertrude continues to receive awards. In 1991, she became the first woman member of the National Inventors Hall of Fame. This is an extraordinary honor, given to very few people. Gertrude joins other inventors like Thomas Edison and George Washington Carver. Receiving this honor made Gertrude feel a little uncomfortable. She really had never thought of herself as an inventor. Gertrude did feel, however, that it was about time that a woman inventor was recognized with the honor.

Gertrude and George celebrated with their colleagues at Burroughs Wellcome after receiving the Nobel Prize in 1988.

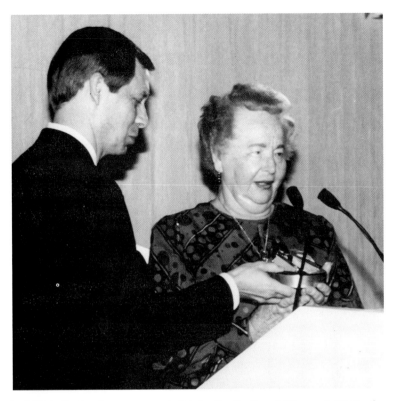

In 1991, Gertrude was accepted into the National Women's Hall of Fame. She was the forty-seventh woman recognized with the honor.

In 1991, Gertrude became the forty-seventh person to be named to the National Women's Hall of Fame, which honors the achievements of women.

One other important honor that was very late in coming to Gertrude was an invitation to become a member of the National Academy of Sciences. If Gertrude had been a man, her achievements would most likely have led to membership much sooner. But Gertrude does not hold grudges. She looks forward to the future, when more and more women will be a part of the scientific community.

Passing on the Research Torch

In the early part of her life, Gertrude focused her attention on doing research to benefit others. Today, she is working toward helping others to follow in her footsteps. As she herself commented, "I've reached a stage where I teach and I'm ready to pass the research torch on to others to carry."

In 1991, President George Bush acknowledged Gertrude's extensive contributions to medical research by awarding her the National Medal of Science.

To fulfill this new goal, Gertrude teaches at Duke University in Durham, North Carolina, and at the University of North Carolina at Chapel Hill. She likes being able to get out to talk with students, to inspire in them a love of science like her own. She is as excited by their curiosity and wonder as they are.

Working with children is also important to Gertrude. Her hopes for these students as future scientists are high. "They love to discover," she says of the little ones. "If you can just keep them at it and make them realize what it is like, they will go into science."

Thanks to the wonderful example of Gertrude Belle Elion, many young people will now have a role model to look up to when they consider what sort of future they might have. Exceptional inventiveness, inspiration, and discipline have made Gertrude Elion one of the most important and remarkable scientists of the twentieth century. Her work as a teacher and researcher will most certainly continue to affect our lives far into the future.

GLOSSARY

chemist A person who investigates the composition and properties of chemical substances.

compound A substance composed of two or more chemical elements, such as water, which is made up of the elements hydrogen and oxygen.

dissection Cutting open a dead body to examine it.

graft Living tissue that is removed from one part of the body and placed in another part of the body.

leukemia A disease that affects the body's tissues and blood; a form of cancer.

patent A kind of government license that allows a person to make, use, or sell an invention for a certain period of time.

pharmaceutical A drug to treat disease.

physicist A scientist who deals with matter and energy in terms of motion and force.

physiology The science that deals with the functions of life and living matter.

purine A chemical compound found in human cells.

suture A thread used to sew parts of the body after an operation.

transplant To replace a diseased organ with a healthy organ from another body.

FOR FURTHER READING

Aaseng, Nathan. *Inventors: Nobel Prizes in Chemistry, Physics, and Medicine.* Minneapolis: Lerner, 1988.

Parker, Steve. *Chemistry.* New York: Franklin Watts, 1990.

Veglahn, Nancy. *Women Scientists.* New York: Facts on File, 1992.

AIDS, 32, 35
A&P, 24
AZT, 32, 35

Burroughs Wellcome, 5–6,
    27, 28, 30, 35, 36
    See also Gertrude Belle
    Elion.
Bush, George, 44

Carver, George Washington,
    42
Chapel Hill, North Carolina,
    36
Curie, Madame, 17, 28, 38

de Kruif, Paul, 12
Duke University. See
    Gertrude Belle Elion.

Edison, Thomas, 42
Elion, Gertrude Belle
    awards and honors, 5, 9,
        40–41, 42, 43, 44
    birth, 10
    at Burroughs Wellcome,
        5–6, 25–26, 27–38,
        39–40, 42
    childhood, 10, 12–16
    at Duke University, 45

at Hunter College, 15, 16,
    17–18, 20, 21
at New York University,
    22–23
at Polytechnic University,
    30–31
retirement, 39
at University of North
    Carolina at Chapel Hill,
    45
Elion, Herbert (brother),
    10, 16
Elion, Mr. (father), 10, 16
Elion, Mrs. (mother), 10, 11
Empirin, 25

Falco, Elvira, 28–29

Hitchings, George, 6, 26,
    27–29, 30, 33, 35, 37,
    40, 41, 42
Hunter College. See Gertrude
    Belle Elion.

Imuran, 6–9, 35

Johnson & Johnson, 24

Leukemia, 29, 31, 33
Lollipop (dog), 9

Microbe Hunters, 12

National Academy of
Sciences, 43
National Cancer Advisory
Board, 39
National Inventors Hall of
Fame, 5, 42
National Medal of Science, 44
National Women's Hall of
Fame, 43
New York Hospital School of
Nursing, 22
New York University. *See*
Gertrude Belle Elion.
Nobel Prize, 9, 40–41, 42

North Carolina at Chapel
Hill, University of. *See*
Gertrude Belle Elion.

Otis, Dr., 17, 18

Pasteur, Louis, 28
Polytechnic University. *See*
Gertrude Belle Elion.
Purinethol, 31, 35

Wellcome, Henry, 27
World Health Organization,
39
World War II, 19, 23

Photo Credits:
Cover: Courtesy of Burroughs Wellcome; p. 4: Courtesy of Burroughs Wellcome; p. 6: Courtesy of Burroughs Wellcome; p. 8: Courtesy of Burroughs Wellcome; p. 11: Courtesy of Burroughs Wellcome; p. 13: Courtesy of Burroughs Wellcome; p. 16: Courtesy of Burroughs Wellcome; p. 21: Courtesy of Burroughs Wellcome; p. 25: Courtesy of Burroughs Wellcome; p. 29: Courtesy of Burroughs Wellcome; p. 32: Courtesy of Burroughs Wellcome; p. 33: Courtesy of Burroughs Wellcome; p. 34: Courtesy of Burroughs Wellcome; p. 37: Courtesy of Burroughs Wellcome; p. 42: Courtesy of Burroughs Wellcome; p. 43: Courtesy of Burroughs Wellcome; p. 44: Courtesy of Burroughs Wellcome.

Illustrations by Dick Smolinski.

Special thanks to Kathy Bartlett at Burroughs Wellcome.